Oversized Knits

Jumbo weight yarn combined with 11 easy designs make Oversized Knits super fast and super fun! Choose from fashion accessories or home décor, grab your needles and knit!

D0777695

LEISURE ARTS, INC.
Maumelle, Arkansas

BLANKET

EASY

Finished Size: 46½" x 70½" (118 cm x 179 cm)

SHOPPING LIST
Yarn (Jumbo Weight) [7]
[10 ounces, 29 yards
(283 grams, 26 meters) per skein]:
☐ 12 skeins
Knitting Needles
36" (91.5 cm) Circular,
☐ Size 50 (25 mm)
   or size needed for gauge

GAUGE INFORMATION

In Stockinette Stitch
  (knit one row, purl one row),
  3 sts = 4" (10 cm);
  4 rows = 3¾" (9.5 cm)

Hint: It may be easier to knit the Body using two circular needles as straight needles. Begin by casting all stitches onto one circular needle, then work each row using the empty needle.

BODY

Cast on 35 sts; do **not** join.

Rows 1 and 2: Knit across.

Row 3 (Right side)**:** K1, P1, (K7, P1) across to last st, K1.

Row 4: K2, P7, (K1, P7) across to last 2 sts, K2.

Row 5: K1, P2, K5, (P3, K5) across to last 3 sts, P2, K1.

Row 6: K3, (P5, K3) across.

Row 7: K1, P3, K3, (P5, K3) across to last 4 sts, P3, K1.

Row 8: K4, P3, (K5, P3) across to last 4 sts, K4.

Row 9: K1, P4, K1, (P7, K1) across to last 5 sts, P4, K1.

Rows 10 and 11: K5, P1, (K7, P1) across to last 5 sts, K5.

Row 12: K1, P4, K1, (P7, K1) across to last 5 sts, P4, K1.

Row 13: K4, P3, (K5, P3) across to last 4 sts, K4.

Row 14: K1, P3, K3, (P5, K3) across to last 4 sts, P3, K1.

Row 15: K3, (P5, K3) across.

Row 16: K1, P2, K5, (P3, K5) across to last 3 sts, P2, K1.

Row 17: K2, P7, (K1, P7) across to last 2 sts, K2.

Rows 18 and 19: K1, P1, (K7, P1) across to last st, K1.

Rows 20-73: Repeat Rows 4-19, 3 times; then repeat Rows 4-9 once **more**.

Rows 74 and 75: Knit across.

Bind off all sts in **knit**.

PILLOW EASY

Finished Size: 21" (53.5 cm) diameter

SHOPPING LIST
Yarn (Jumbo Weight)
[3.5 ounces, 16.5 yards
(100 grams, 15 meters) per skein]:
☐ 5 skeins
Knitting Needles
Double pointed (set of 5),
☐ Size 50 (25 mm)
    or size needed for gauge
36" (91.5 cm) Circular,
☐ Size 50 (25 mm)
Additional Supplies
☐ 21" (53.5 cm) diameter round pillow form
☐ Split-ring marker
☐ Yarn needle

GAUGE INFORMATION

In Stockinette Stitch
 (knit one row, purl one row),
 3 sts and 4 rows = 4" (10 cm)

TECHNIQUES USED

• K1 tbl *(Fig. 3, page 44)*
• P1 tbl *(Fig. 4, page 44)*
• YO *(Figs. 7a & b, page 45)*

Change to circular needle when there are too many stitches for double pointed needles.

FRONT

Cast on 8 sts.

Divide sts onto 4 needles *(see Using Double Pointed Needles, page 43)*; place marker to indicate the beginning of the round *(see Markers, page 42)*.

Rnd 1 (Right side)**:** Knit around.

Rnd 2: (K1, YO) around: 16 sts.

Rnd 3: (K1, K1 tbl) around.

Rnd 4: (K2, YO) around: 24 sts.

Rnd 5: (K2, K1 tbl) around.

Rnd 6: (K3, YO) around: 32 sts.

Rnd 7: (K3, K1 tbl) around.

Rnd 8: (K4, YO) around: 40 sts.

Rnd 9: (K4, K1 tbl) around.

Rnd 10: Knit around.

Bind off all sts in **knit**.

BACK

Cast on 8 sts.

Divide sts onto 4 needles; place marker to indicate the beginning of the round.

Rnd 1 (Right side)**:** Knit around.

Rnd 2: (YO, K1) around: 16 sts.

Rnd 3: (K1, P1 tbl) around.

Rnd 4: (K1, P1, YO) around: 24 sts.

Rnd 5: (K1, P1, P1 tbl) around.

Rnd 6: (K1, P2, YO) around: 32 sts.

Rnd 7: (K1, P2, P1 tbl) around.

Rnd 8: (K1, P3, YO) around: 40 sts.

Rnd 9: (K1, P3, P1 tbl) around.

Rnd 10: (K1, P4) around.

Bind off all sts in **knit**.

With **wrong** sides of Front and Back together, sew pieces together inserting pillow form before closing.

CAPELET  **EASY**

SHOPPING LIST
Yarn (Jumbo Weight)
[10 ounces, 29 yards
(283 grams, 26 meters) per skein]:
- ☐ 3{4-4} skeins

Knitting Needles
36" (91.5 cm) Circular,
- ☐ Size 50 (25 mm)
    or size needed for gauge

Additional Supplies
- ☐ Split-ring marker
- ☐ Yarn needle

Sizes: Small/Medium
{Large/XL-2XL/3XL}
Bottom Circumference:
45{50¾-53}"/114.5{129-134.5} cm
Length: 16" (40.5 cm)

Size Note: We have printed the instructions for
the sizes in different colors to make it easier for
you to find:
- Size Small/Medium in Blue
- Size Large/XL in Pink
- Size 2XL/3XL in Green
Instructions in Black apply to all sizes.

GAUGE INFORMATION

In Stockinette Stitch
(knit one row, purl one row),
3 sts and 4 rows = 4" (10 cm)

TECHNIQUE USED

• K2 tog *(Fig. 9, page 46)*

CAPELET

With circular needle, cast on
34{38-40} sts *(see Using A Circular
Needle, page 42)*; place marker
to indicate the beginning of the
round *(see Markers, page 42)*.

Rnds 1 and 2: (K1, P1) around.

Rnds 3-9: Knit around.

Rnd 10 (Right side)**:** K2 tog,
K 13{15-16}, K2 tog twice,
K 13{15-16}, K2 tog: 30{34-36} sts.

**Size Small/Medium{2XL/3XL}
Only**
Rnd 11: (K2 tog, K1) around:
20{24} sts.

Size Large/XL Only
Rnd 11: K2 tog twice, (K1, K2 tog)
around: 22 sts.

All Sizes
Bind off all sts in knit; do **not** cut
yarn.

COLLAR

Working through back loop only,
pick up one st in each bound off
st around *(Fig. 11, page 47)*; place
marker to indicate the beginning
of the round: 20{22-24} sts.

Rnds 1-3: (K1, P1) around.

Bind off all sts in pattern.

CHILD'S HAT & SCARF

EASY

SHOPPING LIST

Yarn (Jumbo Weight) 7
[8.8 ounces, 21 yards
(250 grams, 19 meters) per skein]:
☐ 2 skeins

Knitting Needles
Double pointed (set of 5),
☐ Size 50 (25 mm)
   or size needed for gauge

Additional Supplies
☐ Split-ring marker
☐ Yarn needle

GAUGE INFORMATION

In Stockinette Stitch
  (knit one row, purl one row),
  3 sts and 4 rows = 4" (10 cm)

TECHNIQUE USED

• K2 tog (*Fig. 9, page 46*)

HAT

Finished Sizes: Small{Medium}
Head Circumference:
  16{18¾}"/40.5{47.5} cm

Size Note: We have printed
the instructions for the sizes in
different colors to make it easier
for you to find:
• Size Small in Blue
• Size Medium in Pink
Instructions in Black apply to
both sizes.

Cast on 12{14} sts.

Divide sts onto 4 needles (*see
Using Double Pointed Needles,
page 43*); place a split-ring
marker to indicate the beginning
of the round (*see Markers,
page 42*).

Rnds 1-6: Knit around.

Rnd 7: K2 tog around: 6{7} sts.

Cut yarn, leaving a long end for
sewing.

Thread yarn needle with the end
and slip the remaining sts onto
the yarn needle and yarn; pull
tightly to close the hole and
secure end.

POM-POM

Cut a piece of cardboard 3½" (9 cm) square.
Wind yarn around the cardboard approximately 10 times *(Fig. A)*.
Carefully slip the yarn off the cardboard and firmly tie an 18"
(45.5 cm) length of yarn around the middle *(Fig. B)*. Leave yarn ends
long enough to attach the pom-pom. Cut the loops on both ends
and trim the pom-pom into a smooth ball *(Fig. C)*.

Fig. A	**Fig. B**	**Fig. C**

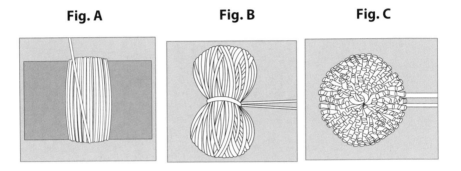

Attach pom-pom to top of Hat.

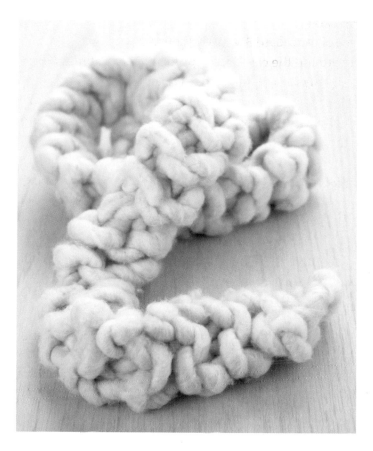

SCARF

Finished Size: 2½" wide x 52" long (6.25 cm x 132 cm)

Cast on 2 sts.

Work in Garter Stitch (knit every row) until piece measures approximately 51" (129.5 cm) from cast on edge.

Last Row: K2, with left needle bring first stitch over the second stitch and off the needle; cut the yarn and bring it up through the last stitch, pulling to tighten.

FOOTSTOOL COVER ◖■◻⬭ EASY

Finished Size: 12" (30.5 cm) diameter

SHOPPING LIST

Yarn (Jumbo Weight) (🌀7)
[3.5 ounces, 16.5 yards
(100 grams, 15 meters) per skein]:
☐ 3 skeins

Knitting Needles

36" (91.5 cm) Circular,
☐ Size 50 (25 mm) **or** size needed for gauge
Double pointed (set of 5),
☐ Size 50 (25 mm)

Additional Supplies

☐ Split-ring marker
☐ Yarn needle

GAUGE INFORMATION

In Garter Stitch (knit each row),
 5 sts and 7 rows = 4" (10 cm)

TECHNIQUES USED

• M1 *(Figs. 6a & b, page 45)*
• K2 tog *(Fig. 9, page 46)*

COVER

Change to double pointed needles when there are too few sts to use the circular needle.

With circular needle, cast on 32 sts *(see Using A Circular Needle, page 42)*; place a marker to indicate the beginning of the round *(see Markers, page 42)*.

Rnd 1: Knit around.

Rnd 2: K2, M1, (K6, M1) around: 38 sts.

Rnd 3: Purl around.

Rnd 4: ★ K3, (K2 tog, K2) 4 times; repeat from ★ once **more**: 30 sts.

Rnd 5: Purl around.

Rnd 6: (K1, K2 tog) around: 20 sts.

Rnd 7: Purl around.

Rnd 8: (K3, K2 tog) around: 16 sts.

Rnd 9: Purl around.

Rnd 10: (K2, K2 tog) around: 12 sts.

Rnd 11: Purl around.

Rnd 12: K2 tog around: 6 sts.

Cut yarn, leaving a long end for sewing.

Thread yarn needle with the end and slip the remaining sts onto the yarn needle and yarn; pull **tightly** to close the hole and secure end.

HOODED COWL
◾◼☐☐☐ **EASY**

Finished Size: Child

SHOPPING LIST
Yarn (Jumbo Weight) 🔸**7**
[8.8 ounces, 21 yards
(250 grams, 19 meters)
per skein]:
☐ 2 skeins

Knitting Needles
36" (91.5 cm) Circular,
☐ Size 50 (25 mm)
or size needed for gauge

Additional Supplies
☐ 1³/₁₆" (30 mm) buttons - 2
☐ Split-ring markers - 2
☐ Stitch holder
☐ Yarn needle
☐ Sewing needle and
matching thread

GAUGE INFORMATION
In Stockinette Stitch
(knit one row, purl one row),
3 sts and 4 rows = 4" (10 cm)

TECHNIQUE USED
• Adding New Stitches (*Figs. 8a & b, page 46*)

COWL
FIRST SIDE
Cast on 4 sts.

Row 1: Slip 1 as if to **purl**, P3.

Row 2 (Right side)**:** Knit across.

Rows 3 and 4: Repeat Rows 1 and 2.

Cut yarn and slip sts onto st holder.

SECOND SIDE

Work same as First Side; do **not** cut yarn.

BODY

Row 1: P4, **turn**; add on 14 sts, **turn**; slip First Side sts from st holder onto opposite end of needle, P4: 22 sts.

Row 2: K7, place marker in next st for Ear placement, K6, place marker in next st for Ear placement, knit across.

Rows 3-11: Beginning with a purl row, work in Stockinette Stitch.

Bind off all sts in **knit**, leaving a long end for weaving.

Using long end, weave back seam as follows:
Fold Body in half. With **right** side of both edges facing you and matching stitches, bring the yarn needle from behind the work and through the center of the

first stitch. ★ Bring the yarn needle over the top of the bound off stitches and insert it under both loops on the second side *(Fig. A)*. Bring the yarn needle back over the bound off stitches and insert it under the inverted V of the next stitch *(Fig. B)*. Repeat from ★ across, being careful to maintain even tension.

Fig. A

FIRST EAR

With **right** side facing, pick up one st in marked st and in next 2 sts *(Fig. C)*: 3 sts.

Row 1: Purl across.

Row 2: Knit across.

Cut yarn, leaving a long end for sewing.

Fig. B

Thread yarn needle with the end and slip the sts onto the yarn needle and yarn; pull **tightly** and secure end.

SECOND EAR

Work same as First Ear in second marked st.

Sew buttons to Left Front; use spaces in stitches for buttonholes.

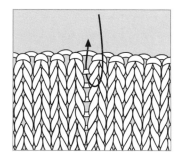

Fig. C

MESSY BUN HAT ▰☐☐⊐ BEGINNER

Head Circumference: 20-21" (51-53.5 cm)

SHOPPING LIST

Yarn (Jumbo Weight) **🎱7**
[8.8 ounces, 21 yards
(250 grams, 19 meters)
per skein]:
- ☐ 1 skein

Knitting Needles

Double pointed (set of 5),
- ☐ Size 50 (25 mm)
  or size needed for gauge

Additional Supplies

- ☐ Split-ring marker

GAUGE INFORMATION

In Stockinette Stitch
(knit one row, purl one row),
3 sts and 4 rows = 4" (10 cm)

TECHNIQUE USED

- K2 tog *(Fig. 9, page 46)*

HAT

Cast on 16 sts.

Divide sts onto 4 needles *(see Using Double Pointed Needles, page 43)*; place marker to indicate the beginning of the round *(see Markers, page 42)*.

Rnds 1-3: Knit around.

Rnd 4: (K2, K2 tog) around:
12 sts.

Rnd 5: Knit around.

Bind off all sts in **knit**.

MUFF  EASY

Finished Size:
14¾" circumference x 13" long (37.5 cm x 33 cm)

SHOPPING LIST

Yarn (Jumbo Weight) 🧶**7**
[5.29 ounces, 46 yards
(150 grams, 42 meters)
per skein]:
☐ 1 skein

Knitting Needles

Double pointed (set of 5),
☐ Size 19 (15 mm)
   or size needed for gauge

Additional Supplies

☐ Split-ring marker

GAUGE INFORMATION

In Stockinette Stitch (knit one row, purl one row),
6 sts and 9 rows = 4" (10 cm)

TECHNIQUES USED

- K2 tog *(Fig. 9, page 46)*
- M1 *(Figs. 6a & b, page 45)*

RIBBING

Cast on 18 sts.

Divide sts onto 4 needles *(see Using Double Pointed Needles, page 43)*; place marker to indicate the beginning of the round *(see Markers, page 42)*.

Rnds 1-7: (K1, P1) around.

Rnds 2-14: Knit around.

Rnd 15: K2, (K2 tog, K3) around: 18 sts.

RIBBING

Rnds 1-7: (K1, P1) around.

Bind off all sts in pattern.

SCARF EASY

Finished Size: 11" wide x 80" long (28 cm x 203 cm)

SHOPPING LIST

Yarn (Jumbo Weight) **JUMBO 7**
[5.29 ounces, 46 yards
(150 grams, 42 meters)
per skein]:
☐ 5 skeins

Knitting Needles

Straight,
☐ Size 19 (15 mm)
   or size needed for gauge

GAUGE INFORMATION

In Stockinette Stitch
(knit one row, purl one row),
6 sts and 9 rows = 4" (10 cm)

TECHNIQUES USED

- YO (*Fig. 7a, page 45*)
- K2 tog (*Fig. 9, page 46*)
- SSK (*Figs. 10a-c, page 47*)

BODY

Cast on 18 sts.

Row 1: K2, P 14, K2.

Row 2 (Right side)**:** K2, YO, SSK, K2 tog, ★ YO, K1, YO, SSK, K2 tog; repeat from ★ once **more**, YO, K2.

Rows 3-10: Repeat Rows 1 and 2, 4 times.

Row 11: K2, P 14, K2.

Row 12: Knit across.

Rows 13 and 14: Repeat Rows 11 and 12.

Rows 15-22: Repeat Rows 1 and 2, 4 times.

Rows 23-26: Repeat Rows 11 and 12 twice.

Rows 27-32: Repeat Rows 1 and 2, 3 times.

Rows 33-36: Repeat Rows 11 and 12 twice.

Rows 37-40: Repeat Rows 1 and 2 twice.

Rows 41-44: Repeat Rows 11 and 12 twice.

Rows 45 and 46: Repeat Rows 1 and 2.

Rows 47-130: Repeat Rows 11 and 12, 42 times.

Rows 131 and 132: Repeat Rows 1 and 2.

Rows 133-136: Repeat Rows 11 and 12 twice.

Rows 137-140: Repeat Rows 1 and 2 twice.

Rows 141-144: Repeat Rows 11 and 12 twice.

Rows 145-150: Repeat Rows 1 and 2, 3 times.

Rows 151-154: Repeat Rows 11 and 12 twice.

Rows 155-162: Repeat Rows 1 and 2, 4 times.

Rows 163-166: Repeat Rows 11 and 12 twice.

Rows 167-176: Repeat Rows 1 and 2, 5 times.

Bind off all sts in **knit**.

SLOUCHY HAT ⬤▮▯▯ EASY

SHOPPING LIST

Yarn (Jumbo Weight) 🧶**7**
**[5.29 ounces, 46 yards
(150 grams, 42 meters) per skein]:**
☐ 1{2} skein(s)

Knitting Needles

Double pointed (set of 5),
☐ Size 15 (10 mm) **and**
☐ Size 19 (15 mm) **or** sizes needed for gauge

Additional Supplies

☐ Split-ring marker
☐ Yarn needle

SIZE INFORMATION

Finished Sizes: Small{Medium}
Head Circumference: 18¾{21}"/47.5{53.5} cm

Size Note: We have printed the instructions for the sizes in different colors to make it easier for you to find:
• Size Small in Blue
• Size Medium in Pink
Instructions in Black apply to both sizes.

GAUGE INFORMATION

With larger size needles,
   in Stockinette Stitch
   (knit one row, purl one row),
   6 sts and 9 rows = 4" (10 cm)

TECHNIQUES USED

• Increase *(Figs. 5a & b, page 44)*
• K2 tog *(Fig. 9, page 46)*

RIBBING

With smaller size needles, cast on 28{32} sts.

Divide sts onto 4 needles *(see Using Double Pointed Needles, page 43)*; place marker to indicate the beginning of the round *(see Markers, page 42)*.

Rnds 1-3: (K1, P1) around.

BODY

Change to larger size needles.

Rnd 1 (Right side)**:** Knit around increasing 12{8} sts evenly spaced: 40 sts.

Rnds 2-11: Knit around.

SHAPING

Rnd 1: (K3, K2 tog) around: 32 sts.

Rnd 2: Knit around.

Rnd 3: (K2, K2 tog) around: 24 sts.

Rnd 4: Knit around.

Rnd 5: (K1, K2 tog) around: 16 sts.

Rnd 6: Knit around.

Rnd 7: K2 tog around: 8 sts.

Rnd 8: Knit around.

Cut yarn, leaving a long end for sewing.

Thread yarn needle with the end and slip the remaining sts onto the yarn needle and yarn; pull **tightly** to close the hole and secure end.

GENERAL INSTRUCTIONS

ABBREVIATIONS

cm	centimeters
K	knit
M1	make one
mm	millimeters
P	purl
SSK	slip, slip, knit
st(s)	stitch(es)
tog	together
YO	yarn over

SYMBOLS & TERMS

★ — work instructions following ★ as many **more** times as indicated in addition to the first time.

( ) or [ ] — work enclosed instructions **as many** times as specified by the number immediately following **or** contains explanatory remarks.

colon (:) — the number(s) given after a colon at the end of a row or round denote(s) the number of stitches you should have on that row or round.

KNIT TERMINOLOGY	
UNITED STATES	**INTERNATIONAL**
gauge =	tension
bind off =	cast off
yarn over (YO) =	yarn forward (yfwd) **or** yarn around needle (yrn)

■□□□ BEGINNER	Projects for first-time knitters using basic knit and purl stitches. Minimal shaping.
■■□□ EASY	Projects using basic stitches, repetitive stitch patterns, simple color changes, and simple shaping and finishing.
■■■□ INTERMEDIATE	Projects with a variety of stitches, such as basic cables and lace, simple intarsia, double-pointed needles and knitting in the round needle techniques, mid-level shaping and finishing.
■■■■ EXPERIENCED	Projects using advanced techniques and stitches, such as short rows, fair isle, more intricate intarsia, cables, lace patterns, and numerous color changes.

GAUGE

Exact gauge is **essential** for proper size. Before beginning your project, make a sample swatch in the yarn and needle specified in the individual instructions. After completing the swatch, measure it, counting your stitches and rows carefully. If your swatch is larger or smaller than specified, **make another, changing needle size to get the correct gauge**. Keep trying until you find the size needles that will give you the specified gauge.

KNITTING NEEDLES		
UNITED STATES	ENGLISH U.K.	METRIC (mm)
0	13	2
1	12	2.25
2	11	2.75
3	10	3.25
4	9	3.5
5	8	3.75
6	7	4
7	6	4.5
8	5	5
9	4	5.5
10	3	6
10½	2	6.5
11	1	8
13	00	9
15	000	10
17	---	12.75
19	---	15
35	---	19
50	---	25

Yarn Weight Symbol & Names	LACE 0	SUPER FINE 1	FINE 2	LIGHT 3	MEDIUM 4	BULKY 5	SUPER BULKY 6	JUMBO 7
Type of Yarns in Category	Fingering, size 10 crochet thread	Sock, Fingering, Baby	Sport, Baby	DK, Light Worsted	Worsted, Afghan, Aran	Chunky, Craft, Rug	Super Bulky, Roving	Jumbo, Roving
Knit Gauge Ranges in Stockinette St to 4" (10 cm)	33-40 sts**	27-32 sts	23-26 sts	21-24 sts	16-20 sts	12-15 sts	7-11 sts	6 sts and fewer
Advised Needle Size Range	000 to 1	1 to 3	3 to 5	5 to 7	7 to 9	9 to 11	11 to 17	17 and larger

* GUIDELINES ONLY: The chart above reflects the most commonly used gauges and needle sizes for specific yarn categories.

** Lace weight yarns are usually knitted on larger needles to create lacy openwork patterns. Accordingly, a gauge range is difficult to determine. Always follow the gauge stated in your pattern.

MARKERS

When using double pointed or circular needles, a split-ring marker is placed around the first stitch of the round to indicate the beginning of a round. Place a marker as instructed and move it up at the beginning of each round.

USING A CIRCULAR NEEDLE

When you knit a tube, you are going to work around on the outside of the circle, with the **right** side of the knitting facing you.

Using a circular needle, cast on all stitches as instructed. Untwist and straighten the stitches on the needle to be sure that the cast on ridge lies on the inside of the needle and never rolls around the needle.

Hold the needle so that the skein of yarn is attached to the stitch closest to the right hand point. Place a marker on the right hand point to mark the beginning of the round *(Fig. 1)*.

Fig. 1

To begin working in the round, knit the stitches on the left hand point. Continue working each round as instructed without turning the work.

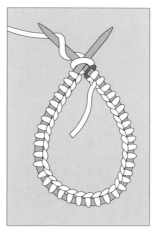

USING DOUBLE POINTED KNITTING NEEDLES

When working a piece that is too small to use a circular knitting needle, double pointed knitting needles are required. Divide the stitches into fourths and slip one-fourth of the stitches onto each of 4 double pointed needles *(Fig. 2a)*, forming a square *(Fig. 2b)*. Do **not** twist the cast on ridge. With the fifth needle, knit across the stitches on the first needle. You will now have an empty needle with which to knit the stitches from the next needle. Work the first stitch of each needle firmly to prevent gaps. Continue working around without turning the work.

Fig. 2a

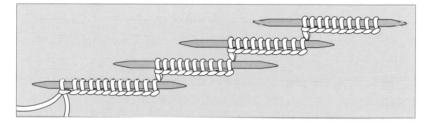

Fig. 2b

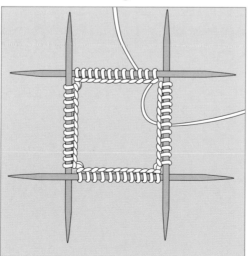

KNIT ONE THROUGH BACK LOOP
(abbreviated K1 tbl)

Insert the right needle into the **back** of the next stitch from **front** to **back** *(Fig. 3)*, then knit the stitch.

Fig. 3

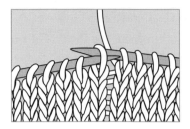

PURL ONE THROUGH BACK LOOP
(abbreviated P1 tbl)

Insert the right needle into the **back** of the next stitch from **back** to **front** *(Fig. 4)*, then purl the stitch.

Fig. 4

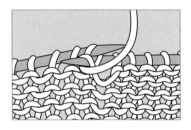

INCREASES
INCREASE

Knit the next stitch but do **not** slip the old stitch off the left needle *(Fig. 5a)*. Insert the right needle into the **back** loop of the **same** stitch and knit it *(Fig. 5b)*, then slip the old stitch off the left needle.

Fig. 5a

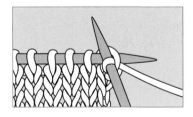

Fig. 5b

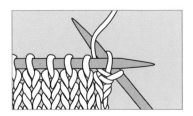

MAKE ONE (abbreviated M1)

Insert the **left** needle under the horizontal strand between the stitches from the front *(Fig. 6a)*. Then knit into the **back** of the strand *(Fig. 6b)*.

Fig. 6a

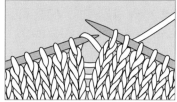

YARN OVER (abbreviated YO)

After a knit stitch, before a knit stitch.

Bring the yarn forward **between** the needles, then back **over** the top of the right hand needle, so that it is now in position to knit the next stitch *(Fig. 7a)*.

After a purl stitch, before a knit stitch.

Take the yarn **over** the right hand needle to the back, so that it is now in position to knit the next stitch *(Fig. 7b)*.

Fig. 6b

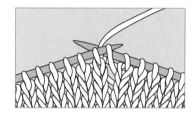

Fig. 7a

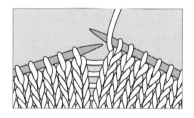

Fig. 7b

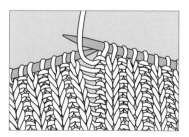

ADDING NEW STITCHES

Insert the right needle into stitch as if to **knit**, yarn over and pull loop through *(Fig. 8a)*, insert the left needle into the loop just worked from **front** to **back** and slip the loop onto the left needle *(Fig. 8b)*. Repeat for required number of stitches.

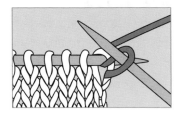

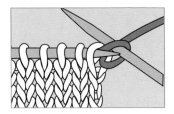

DECREASES
KNIT 2 TOGETHER

(abbreviated K2 tog)

Insert the right needle into the **front** of the first two stitches on the left needle as if to **knit** *(Fig. 9)*, then **knit** them together as if they were one stitch.

Fig. 9

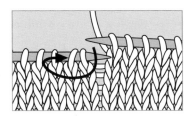

SLIP, SLIP, KNIT
(abbreviated SSK)
Separately slip two stitches as if to **knit** *(Fig. 10a)*. Insert the left needle into the **front** of both slipped stitches *(Fig. 10b)* and then knit them together as if they were one stitch *(Fig. 10c)*.

PICKING UP STITCHES
When instructed to pick up stitches, insert the needle from the **front** to the **back** under back loop only at the edge of the worked piece *(Fig. 11)*. Put the yarn around the needle as if to **knit**, then bring the needle with the yarn back through the stitch to the right side, resulting in a stitch on the needle.

Repeat this along the edge, picking up the required number of stitches.

A crochet hook may be helpful to pull yarn through.

Fig. 10a

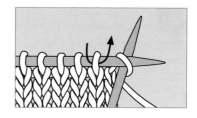

Fig. 10b

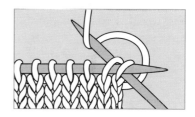

Fig. 10c

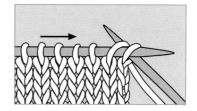

Fig. 11

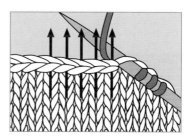

YARN INFORMATION

The items in this book were made using Jumbo Weight Yarn. Any brand of Jumbo Weight Yarn may be used. It is best to refer to the yardage/meters when determining how many balls or skeins to purchase. Remember, to achieve the finished size, it is the GAUGE/TENSION that is important, not the brand of yarn.

For your convenience, listed below are the specific yarns used to create our photography models. Because yarn manufacturers make frequent changes to their product lines, you may sometimes find it necessary to use a substitute yarn or to search for the discontinued product at alternate suppliers (locally or online).

BLANKET
Red Heart® Boutique Irresistible™
#7305 Oatmeal

PILLOW
Premier® Couture Jazz®
#26-02 Milk

CAPELET
Red Heart® Boutique Irresistible™
#7630 Chartreuse

CHILD'S HAT & SCARF
Lion Brand® WOW!®
#102 Mermaids Tale

FOOTSTOOL COVER
Premier® Couture Jazz®
#26-29 Denim

HOODED COWL
Lion Brand® WOW!®
#146 The Fuchsia is bright

MESSY BUN HAT
Lion Brand® WOW!®
#150 Greige

MUFF
Red Heart® Grande™
#0307 Oatmeal

SCARF
Red Heart® Grande™
#0275 Nectar

SLOUCHY HAT
Red Heart® Grande™
#0110 Aran

We have made every effort to ensure that these instructions are accurate and complete. We cannot, however, be responsible for human error, typographical mistakes, or variations in individual work.

Production Team: Instructional/ Technical Editor - Lois J. Long; Senior Graphic Artist - Lora Puls; Photo Stylist - Lori Wenger; and Photographer - Jason Masters.